Spooner Lysander

**Vice Are Not Crimes**

Spooner Lysander

**Vice Are Not Crimes**

ISBN/EAN: 9783744704250

Printed in Europe, USA, Canada, Australia, Japan

Cover: Foto ©Thomas Meinert / pixelio.de

More available books at **www.hansebooks.com**

# THE BEST OF THE OLL #24

## *Lysander Spooner, "Vices are Not Crimes" (1875)*

*"Unless this clear distinction between vices and crimes be made and recognized by the laws, there can be on earth no such thing as individual right, liberty, or property"*

Lysander Spooner (1808-1887)

*The Best of the Online Library of Liberty* <oll.libertyfund.org/title/2465>
*The Best of Bastiat* <oll.libertyfund.org/title/2477>
[March, 2013]

## Editor's Introduction

Lysander Spooner (1808-1887) was a legal theorist, abolitionist, and radical individualist who started his own mail company in order to challenge the monopoly held by the US government. He wrote on the constitutionality of slavery, natural law, trial by jury, intellectual property, paper currency, and banking. Some of his most important works are *An Essay on the Trial by Jury* (1852), *The Unconstitutionality of Slavery* (1860), *No Treason, No. 1, 2, and 6* (1867, 1870), *A Letter to Thomas F. Bayard* (1882), and *A Letter to Grover Cleveland* (1886).

This pamphlet comes from vol. 2 of a two volume compilation of Spooner's shorter works and pamphlets: *The Shorter Works and Pamphlets of Lysander Spooner*.

The distinction Spooner makes between "vice" and "crime" is a crucial one which still has considerable relevance today. In Spooner's day the great vice was alcohol which is why he devotes much space to discussing it. For him, *vices* are acts by which a person harms themselves and their property; *crimes* on the other hand are acts by which a person harms the person or property of *another* person. The latter he believes is the proper concern of the police and the courts; the former is not. According to Spooner's theory of individual liberty it is important that each person be free to make their own mistakes, if necessary, as this is the most important means by which they learn about themselves and the world around them. He wants to see the fullest possible freedom for people so they can "be left free and open for experiment" in the way they live their lives. In other words, to be free to pursue their own idea of happiness.

Although Spooner does not use this term, he is talking about "victimless crimes" when he quotes the Latin legal maxim that "violenti no fit injuria" (to the willing no injury is done). Among these so-called "crimes" he includes consensual sex, prize-fighting, fighting duels, gambling, assisted suicide, and so on. Although American prisons were filled with people who had violated the laws against vices like these, they were not the greatest criminals. He reserved this distinction for governments which fought wars and the men who made the laws which allowed them and their friends "to usurp arbitrary power" legally.

*"The object aimed at in the punishment of crimes is to secure, to each and every man alike, the fullest liberty he possibly can have—consistently with the equal rights of others—to pursue his own happiness, under the guidance of his own judgment, and by the use of his own property. On the other hand, the object aimed at in the punishment of vices, is to deprive every man of his natural right and liberty to pursue his own happiness, under the guidance of his own judgment, and by the use of his own property."*

# Vices are Not Crimes: A Vindication of Moral Liberty (1875)[1]

## I.

*"VICES are those acts by which a man harms himself or his property.*

*Crimes are those acts by which one man harms the person or property of another. Vices are simply the errors which a man makes in his search after his own happiness. Unlike crimes, they imply no malice toward others, and no interference with their persons or property. In vices, the very essence of crime—that is, the design to injure the person or property of another—is wanting."*

VICES are those acts by which a man harms himself or his property.

Crimes are those acts by which one man harms the person or property of another.

Vices are simply the errors which a man makes in his search after his own happiness. Unlike crimes, they imply no malice toward others, and no interference with their persons or property.

In vices, the very essence of crime—that is, the design to injure the person or property of another—is wanting.

It is a maxim of the law that there can be no crime without a criminal intent; that is, without the intent to invade the person or property of another. But no one ever practises a vice with any such criminal intent. He practises his vice for his own happiness solely, and not from any malice toward others.

Unless this clear distinction between vices and crimes be made and recognized by the laws, there can be on earth no such thing as individual right, liberty, or property; no such things as the right of one man to the control of his own person and property, and the corresponding and co-equal rights of another man to the control of his own person and property.

For a government to declare a vice to be a crime, and to punish it as such, is an attempt to falsify the very nature of things. It is as absurd as it would be to declare truth to be falsehood, or falsehood truth.

## II.

EVERY voluntary act of a man's life is either virtuous or vicious. That is to say, it is either in accordance, or in conflict, with those natural laws of matter and mind, on which his physical, mental, and emotional health and well-being depend. In other words, every act of his life tends, on the whole, either to his happiness, or to his unhappiness. No single act in his whole existence is indifferent.

Furthermore, each human being differs in his physical, mental, and emotional constitution, and also in the circumstances by which he is surrounded, from every other human being. Many acts, therefore, that are virtuous, and tend to happiness, in the case of one person, are vicious, and tend to unhappiness, in the case of another person.

Many acts, also, that are virtuous, and tend to happiness, in the case of one man, at one time, and under one set of circumstances, are vicious, and tend to unhappiness, in the case of the same man, at another time, and under other circumstances.

## III.

TO know what actions are virtuous, and what vicious, in other words, to know what actions tend, on the whole, to happiness, and what to unhappiness, —in the case of each and every man, in each and all the conditions in which they may severally be placed, is the profoundest and most complex study to which the greatest human mind ever has been, or ever can be, directed. It is, nevertheless, the constant study to which each and every man—the humblest in intellect as well

[1] Lysander Spooner, *The Shorter Works and Pamphlets of Lysander Spooner, vol. 2 (1862-1884)* (Indianapolis: Liberty Fund, 2010). "Vices are Not Crimes: A Vindication of Moral Liberty." <oll.libertyfund.org/title/2292/217204>.

as the greatest—is *necessarily driven* by the desires and necessities of his own existence. It is also the study in which each and every person, from his cradle to his grave, must necessarily form his own conclusions; because no one else knows or feels, or can know or feel, as he knows and feels, the desires and necessities, the hopes, and fears, and impulses of his own nature, or the pressure of his own circumstances.

## IV.

IT is not often possible to say of those acts that are called vices, that they really are vices, except in *degree*. That is, it is difficult to say of any actions, or courses of action, that are called vices, that they really would have been vices, *if they had stopped short of a certain point*. The question of virtue or vice, therefore, in all such cases, is a question of quantity and degree, and not of the intrinsic character of any single act, by itself. This fact adds to the difficulty, not to say the impossibility, of any one's except each individual for himself drawing any accurate line, or anything like any accurate line, between virtue and vice; that is, of telling where virtue ends, and vice begins. And this is another reason why this whole question of virtue and vice should be left for each person to settle for himself.

## V.

VICES are usually pleasurable, at least for the time being, and often do not disclose themselves as vices, by their effects, until after they have been practised for many years; perhaps for a lifetime. To many, perhaps most, of those who practise them, they do not disclose themselves as vices at all during life. Virtues, on the other hand, often appear so harsh and rugged, they require the sacrifice of so much present happiness, at least, and the results, which alone prove them to be virtues, are often so distant and obscure, in fact, so absolutely invisible to the minds of many, especially of the young, that, from the very nature of things, there can be no universal, or even general, knowledge that they are virtues. In truth, the studies of profound philosophers have been expended if not wholly in vain, certainly with very small results in efforts to draw the lines between the virtues and the vices.

If, then, it be so difficult, so nearly impossible, in most cases, to determine what is, and what is not, vice; and especially if it be so difficult, in nearly all cases, to determine where virtue ends, and vice begins; and if these questions, which no one can really and truly determine for anybody but himself, are not to be left free and open for experiment by all, each person is deprived of the highest of all his rights as a human being, to wit: his right to inquire, investigate, reason, try experiments, judge, and ascertain for himself, what is, to *him*, virtue, and what is, to *him*, vice; in other words, what, on the whole, conduces to *his* happiness, and what, on the whole, tends to his unhappiness. If this great right is not to be left free and open to all, then each man's whole right, as a reasoning human being, to "liberty and the pursuit of happiness," is denied him.

> *"if these questions, which no one can really and truly determine for anybody but himself, are not to be left free and open for experiment by all, each person is deprived of the highest of all his rights as a human being, to wit: his right to inquire, investigate, reason, try experiments, judge, and ascertain for himself, what is, to him, virtue, and what is, to him, vice"*

## VI.

WE all come into the world in ignorance of ourselves, and of everything around us. By a fundamental law of our natures we are all constantly impelled by the desire of happiness, and the fear of pain. But we have everything to learn, as to what will give us happiness, and save us from pain. No two of us are wholly alike, either physically, mentally, or emotionally; or, consequently, in our physical, mental, or emotional requirements for the acquisition of happiness, and the avoidance of unhappiness. No one of us, therefore, can learn this indispensable lesson of happiness and unhappiness, of virtue and vice, for another. Each must learn it for himself. To learn it, he must be at liberty to try all experiments that commend themselves to his judgment. Some of his experiments succeed, and, because they succeed, are called virtues; others fail, and, because they fail, are called vices. He gathers wisdom from his failures, as well as from his successes; from his so-called vices, as from his so-called virtues. He gathers wisdom *as much* from his failures as from his successes; from his so-called vices, as from his so-called virtues. Both are necessary to his acquisition of that knowledge of his own nature, and of the world around him, and of their adaptations or non-adaptations to each other which shall show him how happiness is acquired, and pain avoided. And, unless he can be permitted to try these experiments to his own satisfaction, he is restrained from the acquisition of knowledge, and, consequently, from pursuing the great purpose and duty of his life.

### VII.

A MAN is under no obligation to take anybody's word, or yield to anybody's authority, on a matter so vital to himself, and in regard to which no one else has, or can have, any such interest as he. He *cannot*, if he would, safely rely upon the opinions of other men, because he finds that the opinions of other men do not agree. Certain actions, or courses of action, have been practised by many millions of men, through successive generations, and have been held by them to be, on the whole, conducive to happiness, and therefore virtuous. Other men, in other ages or countries, or under other conditions, have held, as the result of their experience and observation, that these actions tended, on the whole, to unhappiness, and were therefore vicious. The question of virtue or vice, as already remarked in a previous section, has also been, in most minds, a question of degree; that is, of the extent to which certain actions should be carried; and not of the intrinsic character of any single act, by itself. The questions of virtue and vice have therefore been as various, and, in fact, as infinite, as the varieties of mind, body, and condition of the different individuals inhabiting the globe. And the experience of ages has left an infinite number of these questions unsettled. In fact, it can scarcely be said to have settled any of them.

### VIII.

IN the midst of this endless variety of opinion, what man, or what body of men, has the right to say, in regard to any particular action, or course of action,

"*We* have tried this experiment, and determined every question involved in it? *We* have determined it, not only for ourselves, but for all others? And, as to all those who are weaker than we, we will coerce them to act in obedience to our conclusion? *We* will suffer no further experiment or inquiry by any one, and, consequently, no further acquisition of knowledge by anybody?"

Who are the men who have the right to say this? Certainly there are none such. The men who really do say it, are either shameless impostors and tyrants, *who would stop the progress of knowledge*, and usurp absolute control over the minds and bodies of their fellow-men; and are therefore to be resisted instantly, and to the last extent; or they are themselves too ignorant of their own weaknesses, and of their true relations to other men, to be entitled to any other consideration than sheer pity or contempt.

*"The men who really do say it, are either shameless impostors and tyrants, who would stop the progress of knowledge, and usurp absolute control over the minds and bodies of their fellow-men; and are therefore to be resisted instantly, and to the last extent; or they are themselves too ignorant of their own weaknesses, and of their true relations to other men, to be entitled to any other consideration than sheer pity or contempt."*

We know, however, that there are such men as these in the world. Some of them attempt to exercise their power only within a small sphere, to wit, upon their children, their neighbors, their townsmen, and their countrymen. Others attempt to exercise it on a larger scale. For example, an old man at Rome, aided by a few subordinates, attempts to decide all questions of virtue and vice; that is, of truth or falsehood, especially in matters of religion. He claims to know and teach what religious ideas and practices are conducive, or fatal, to a man's happiness, not only in this world, but in that which is to come. He claims to be miraculously inspired for the performance of this work; thus virtually acknowledging, like a sensible man, that nothing short of miraculous inspiration would qualify him for it. This miraculous inspiration, however, has been ineffectual to enable him to settle more than a very few questions. The most important of these are, first, that the highest religious virtue to which common mortals can attain, *is an implicit belief in his (the pope's) infallibility!* and, secondly, that the blackest vices of which they can be guilty are to believe and declare that he is only a man like the rest of them!

It required some fifteen or eighteen hundred years to enable him to reach definite conclusions on these two vital points. Yet it would seem that the first of these must necessarily be preliminary to his settlement of any other questions; because, until his own infallibility is determined, he can authoritatively decide nothing else. He has, however, heretofore attempted or pretended to settle a few others. And he may, perhaps, attempt or pretend to settle a few more in the future, if he shall continue to find anybody to listen to him. But his success, thus far, certainly does not encourage the belief that he will be able to settle all questions of virtue and vice, even in his peculiar department of religion, in time to meet the necessities of mankind. He, or his successors, will undoubtedly be compelled, at no distant day, to acknowledge that he has undertaken a task to which all his miraculous inspiration was inadequate; and that, of necessity, each human being must be left to settle all questions of this kind for himself. And it is not unreasonable to expect that all other popes, in other and lesser spheres, will some time have cause to come to the same conclusion. No one, certainly, not claiming supernatural inspiration, should undertake a task to which obviously nothing less than such inspiration is adequate. And, clearly, no one should surrender his own judgment to the teachings of others, unless he be first convinced that these others have something more than ordinary human knowledge on this subject.

If those persons, who fancy themselves gifted with both the power and the right to define and punish other men's vices, would but turn their thoughts inwardly, they would probably find that they have a great work to do at home; and that, when that shall have been completed, they will be little disposed to do more towards correcting the vices of others, than simply to give to others the results of their experience and observation. In this sphere their labors may possibly be useful; but, in the sphere of infallibility and coercion, they will probably, for well-known reasons, meet with even less success in the future than such men have met with in the past.

## IX.

*"government would be utterly impracticable, if it were to take cognizance of vices, and punish them as crimes... to be consistent, it must take cognizance of all, and punish all impartially. The consequence would be, that everybody would be in prison for his or her vices. There would be no one left outside to lock the doors upon those within. In fact, courts enough could not be found to try the offenders, nor prisons enough built to hold them."*

IT is now obvious, from the reasons already given, that government would be utterly impracticable, if it were to take cognizance of vices, and punish them as crimes. Every human being has his or her vices. Nearly all men have a great many. And they are of all kinds; physiological, mental, emotional; religious, social, commercial, industrial, economical, &c., &c. If government is to take cognizance of any of these vices, and punish them as crimes, then, to be consistent, it must take cognizance of all, and punish all impartially. The consequence would be, that everybody would be in prison for his or her vices. There would be no one left outside to lock the doors upon those within. In fact, courts enough could not be found to try the offenders, nor prisons enough built to hold them. All human industry in the acquisition of knowledge, and even in acquiring the means of subsistence, would be arrested; for we should all be under constant trial or imprisonment for our vices. But even if it were possible to imprison all the vicious, our knowledge of human nature tells us that, as a general rule, they would be far more vicious in prison than they ever have been out of it.

## X.

A GOVERNMENT that shall punish all vices impartially is so obviously an impossibility, that nobody was ever found, or ever will be found, foolish enough to propose it. The most that any one proposes is, that government shall punish some one, or at most a few, of what he esteems the grossest of them. But this discrimination is an utterly absurd, illogical, and tyrannical one. What right has any body of men to say, "The vices of other men we will punish; but our own vices nobody shall punish? We will restrain other men from seeking their own happiness, according to their own notions of it; but nobody shall restrain us from seeking our own happiness, according to our own notions of it? We will restrain other men from acquiring any experimental knowledge of what is conducive or necessary to their own happiness; but nobody shall restrain us from acquiring an experimental knowledge of what is conducive or necessary to our own happiness?"

Nobody but knaves or blockheads ever thinks of making such absurd assumptions as these. And yet, evidently, it is only upon such assumptions that anybody can claim the right to punish the vices of others, and at the same time claim exemption from punishment for his own.

## XI.

SUCH a thing as a government, formed by voluntary association, would never have been thought of, if the object proposed had been the punishment of all vices, impartially; because nobody wants such an institution, or would voluntarily submit to it. But a government, formed by voluntary association, for the punishment of all *crimes*, is a reasonable matter; because everybody wants protection for himself against all crimes by others, and also acknowledges the justice of his own punishment, if he commits a crime.

## XII.

IT is a natural impossibility that a government should have a right to punish men for their *vices*; because it is impossible that a government should have any rights, except such as the individuals composing it had previously had, as *individuals*. They could not delegate to a government any rights which they did not themselves possess. They could not *contribute* to the government any rights, except such as they themselves possessed as individuals. Now, nobody but a fool or an impostor pretends that he, *as an individual*, has a right to punish other men for their vices. But anybody and everybody have a natural right, *as individuals*, to punish other men for their crimes; for everybody has a natural right, not only to defend his own person and property against aggressors, but also to go to the assistance and defence of everybody else, whose person or property is invaded. The natural right of each individual to defend his own person and property against an aggressor, and to go to the assistance and defence of every one else whose person or property is invaded, is a right without which men could not exist on the earth. And government has no rightful existence, except in so far as it embodies, and is limited by, this natural right of individuals. But the idea that each man has a natural right to sit in judgment on all his neighbor's actions, and decide what are virtues, and what are vices, that is, what contribute to that neighbor's happiness, and what do not,—and to punish him for all that do not contribute to it, is what no one ever had the impudence or folly to assert. It is only those who claim that government has some rightful power, *which no individual or individuals ever did, or ever could, delegate to it*, that claim that government has any rightful power to punish vices.

It will do for a pope or a king who claims to have received direct authority from Heaven, to rule over his fellow-men—to claim the right, as the vicegerent of God, to punish men for their vices; but it is a sheer and utter absurdity for any government, claiming to derive its power wholly from the grant of the governed, to claim any such power; because everybody knows that the governed never would grant it. For them to grant it would be an absurdity, because it would be granting away their own right to seek their own happiness; since to grant away their right to judge of what will be for their happiness, is to grant away all their right to pursue their own happiness.

## XIII.

WE can now see how simple, easy, and reasonable a matter is a government for the punishment of *crimes*, as compared with one for the punishment of *vices*.

*Crimes* are few, and easily distinguished from all other acts; and mankind are generally agreed as to what acts are crimes. Whereas vices are innumerable; and no two persons are agreed, except in comparatively few cases, as to what are vices. Furthermore, everybody wishes to be protected, in his person and property, against the aggressions of other men. But nobody *wishes* to be protected, either in his person or property, against himself; because it is contrary to the fundamental laws of human nature itself, that any one should wish to harm himself. He only wishes to promote his own happiness, and to be his own judge as to what will promote, and does promote, his own happiness. This is what every one wants, and has a right to, as a human being. And though we all make many mistakes, and necessarily must make them, from the imperfection of our knowledge, yet these mistakes are no argument against the right; because they all tend to give us the very knowledge we need, and are in pursuit of, and can get in no other way.

The object aimed at in the punishment of *crimes*, therefore, is not only wholly different from, but it is directly opposed to, that aimed at in the punishment of *vices*.

*"The object aimed at in the punishment of crimes is to secure, to each and every man alike, the fullest liberty he possibly can have—consistently with the equal rights of others—to pursue his own happiness, under the guidance of his own judgment, and by the use of his own property. On the other hand, the object aimed at in the punishment of vices, is to deprive every man of his natural right and liberty to pursue his own happiness, under the guidance of his own judgment, and by the use of his own property."*

The object aimed at in the punishment of *crimes* is to *secure*, to each and every man alike, the fullest liberty he possibly can have consistently with the equal rights of others to pursue his own happiness, under the guidance of his own judgment, and by the use of his own property. On the other hand, the object aimed at in the punishment of *vices*, is to *deprive* every man of his natural right and liberty to pursue his own happiness, under the guidance of his own judgment, and by the use of his own property.

These two objects, then, are directly opposed to each other. They are as directly opposed to each other as are light and darkness, or as truth and falsehood, or as liberty and slavery. They are utterly incompatible with each other; and to suppose the two to be embraced in one and the same government, is an absurdity, an impossibility. It is to suppose the objects of a government to be to commit crimes, and to prevent crimes; to destroy individual liberty, and to secure individual liberty.

### XIV.

FINALLY, on this point of individual liberty: Every man *must necessarily* judge and determine for himself as to what is conducive and necessary to, and what is destructive of, his own well-being; because, if he omits to perform this task for himself, nobody else *can* perform it for him. And nobody else will even attempt to perform it for him, except in very few cases. Popes, and priests, and kings will assume to perform it for him, in certain cases, if permitted to do so. But they will, in general, perform it only in so far as they can minister to their own vices and crimes, by doing it. They will, in general, perform it only in so far as they can make him their fool and their slave. Parents, with better motives, no doubt, than the others, too often attempt the same work. But in so far as they practise coercion, or restrain a child from anything not really and seriously dangerous to himself, they do him a harm, rather than a good. It is a law of Nature that to get knowledge, and to incorporate that knowledge into his own being, each individual must get it for himself. Nobody, not even his parents, can tell him the nature of fire, so that he will really know it. He must himself experiment with it, *and be burnt by it*, before he can know it.

Nature knows, a thousand times better than any parent, what she designs each individual for, what knowledge he requires, and how he must get it. She knows that her own processes for communicating that knowledge are not only the best, but the only ones that can be effectual.

The attempts of parents to make their children virtuous are generally little else than attempts to keep them in ignorance of vice. They are little else than attempts to teach their children to know and prefer truth, by keeping them in ignorance of falsehood. They are little else than attempts to make them seek and appreciate health, by keeping them in ignorance of disease, and of everything that will cause disease. They are little else than attempts to make their children love the light, by keeping them in ignorance of darkness. In short, they are little else than attempts to make their children happy, by keeping them in ignorance of everything that causes them unhappiness.

*"to practise coercion in matters of which the children are reasonably competent to judge for themselves, is only an attempt to keep them in ignorance. And this is as much a tyranny, and as much a violation of the children's right to acquire knowledge for themselves, and such knowledge as they desire, as is the same coercion when practised upon older persons"*

In so far as parents can really aid their children in the latter's search after happiness, by simply giving them the results of their (the parents') own reason and experience, it is all very well, and is a natural and appropriate duty. But to practise coercion in matters of which the children are reasonably competent to judge for themselves, is only an attempt to keep them in ignorance. And this is as much a tyranny, and as much a violation of the children's right to acquire knowledge for themselves, and such knowledge as they desire, as is the same coercion when practised upon older persons. Such coercion, practised upon children, is a denial of their right to develop the faculties that Nature has given them, and to be what Nature designs them to be.

It is a denial of their right to themselves, and to the use of their own powers. It is a denial of their right to acquire the most valuable of all knowledge, to wit, the knowledge that Nature, the great teacher, stands ready to impart to them.

The results of such coercion are not to make the children wise or virtuous, but to make them ignorant, and consequently weak and vicious; and to perpetuate through them, from age to age, the ignorance, the superstitions, the vices, and the crimes of the parents. This is proved by every page of the world's history.

Those who hold opinions opposite to these, are those whose false and vicious theologies, or whose own vicious general ideas, have taught them that the human race are naturally given to evil, rather than good; to the false, rather than the true; that mankind do not naturally turn their eyes to the light; that they love darkness, rather than light; and that they find their happiness only in those things that tend to their misery.

XV.

BUT these men, who claim that government shall use its power to prevent vice, will say, or are in the habit of saying, "We acknowledge the right of an individual to seek his own happiness in his own way, and consequently to be as vicious as he pleases; we only claim that government shall prohibit the sale to him of those articles by which he ministers to his vice."

The answer to this is, that the simple sale of any article whatever  independently of the use that is to be made of the article  is legally a perfectly innocent act. The quality of the act of sale depends wholly upon the quality of the use for which the thing is sold. If the use of anything is virtuous and lawful, then the sale of it, *for that use*, is virtuous and lawful. If the use is vicious, then the sale of it, *for that use*, is vicious. If the use is criminal, then the sale of it, *for that use*, is criminal. The seller is, at most, only an accomplice in the use that is to be made of the article sold, whether the use be virtuous, vicious, or criminal. Where the use is criminal, the seller is an accomplice in the crime, and punishable as such. But where the use is only vicious, the seller is only an accomplice in the vice, and is not punishable.

9

## XVI.

BUT it will be asked, "Is there no right, on the part of government, to arrest the progress of those who are bent on self-destruction?"

The answer is, that government has no rights whatever in the matter, so long as these so-called vicious persons remain sane, *compos mentis*, capable of exercising reasonable discretion and self-control; because, so long as they do remain sane, they must be allowed to judge and decide for themselves whether their so-called vices really are vices; whether they really are leading them to destruction; and whether, on the whole, they will go there or not. When they shall become insane, *non compos mentis*, incapable of reasonable discretion or self-control, their friends or neighbors, or the government, must take care of them, and protect them from harm, and against all persons who would do them harm, in the same way as if their insanity had come upon them from any other cause than their supposed vices.

*"Men and women may be addicted to very gross vices, and to a great many of them,—such as gluttony, drunkenness, prostitution, gambling, prize-fighting, tobacco-chewing, smoking, and snuffing, opium-eating, corset-wearing, idleness, waste of property, avarice, hypocrisy, &c., &c.,—and still be sane, compos mentis, capable of reasonable discretion and self-control, within the meaning of the law."*

But because a man is supposed, by his neighbors, to be on the way to self-destruction, from his vices, it does not, therefore, follow that he is insane, *non compos mentis*, incapable of reasonable discretion and self-control, within the legal meaning of those terms. Men and women may be addicted to very gross vices, and to a great many of them,—such as gluttony, drunkenness, prostitution, gambling, prize-fighting, tobacco-chewing, smoking, and snuffing, opium-eating, corset-wearing, idleness, waste of property, avarice, hypocrisy, &c., &c., and still be sane, *compos mentis*, capable of reasonable discretion and self-control, within the meaning of the law. And so long as they are sane, they must be permitted to control themselves and their property, and to be their own judges as to where their vices will finally lead them. It may be hoped by the lookers-on, in each individual case, that the vicious person will see the end to which he is tending, and be induced to turn back. But, if he chooses to go on to what other men call destruction, he must be permitted to do so. And all that can be said of him, so far as this life is concerned, is, that he made a great mistake in his search after happiness, and that others will do well to take warning by his fate. As to what may be his condition in another life, that is a theological question with which the law, in this world, has no more to do than it has with any other theological question, touching men's condition in a future life.

If it be asked how the question of a vicious man's sanity or insanity is to be determined? the answer is, that it is to be determined by the same kinds of evidence as is the sanity or insanity of those who are called virtuous; and not otherwise. That is, by the same kinds of evidence by which the legal tribunals determine whether a man should be sent to an asylum for lunatics, or whether he is competent to make a will, or otherwise dispose of his property. Any doubt must weigh in favor of his sanity, as in all other cases, and not of his insanity.

If a person really does become insane, *non compos mentis*, incapable of reasonable discretion or self-control, it is then a crime, on the part of other men, to give to him or sell to him, the means of self-injury.[1] And such a crime is to be punished like any other crime.

There are no crimes more easily punished, no cases in which juries would be more ready to convict, than those where a sane person should sell or give to an insane one any article with which the latter was likely to injure himself.

## XVII.

BUT it will be said that some men are made, by their vices, dangerous to other persons; that a drunkard, for example, is sometimes quarrelsome and dangerous toward his family or others. And it will be asked, "Has the law nothing to do in such a case?"

The answer is, that if, either from drunkenness or any other cause, a man be really dangerous, either to his family or to other persons, not only himself may be rightfully restrained, so far as the safety of other persons requires, but all other persons who know or have reasonable grounds to believe him dangerous may also be restrained from selling or giving to him anything that they have reason to suppose will make him dangerous.

But because one man becomes quarrelsome and dangerous after drinking spirituous liquors, and because it is a crime to give or sell liquor to such a man, it does not follow at all that it is a crime to sell liquors to the hundreds and thousands of other persons, who are not made quarrelsome or dangerous by drinking them. Before a man can be convicted of crime in selling liquor to a dangerous man, it must be shown that the *particular man*, to whom the liquor was sold, was dangerous; and also that the seller knew, or had reasonable grounds to suppose, that the man would be made dangerous by drinking it.

The presumption of law is, in all cases, that the sale is innocent; and the burden of proving it criminal, in any particular case, rests upon the government. *And that particular case must be proved criminal, independently of all others.*

Subject to these principles, there is no difficulty in convicting and punishing men for the sale or gift of any article to a man, who is made dangerous to others by the use of it.

XVIII.

BUT it is often said that some vices are nuisances (public or private), and that nuisances can be abated and punished.

It is true that anything that is really and legally a nuisance (either public or private) can be abated and punished. But it is not true that the mere private vices of one man are, in any legal sense, nuisances to another man, or to the public.

No act of one person can be a nuisance to another, unless it in some way obstructs or interferes with that other's safe and quiet use or enjoyment of what is rightfully his own.

Whatever obstructs a public highway, is a nuisance, and may be abated and punished. But a hotel where liquors are sold, a liquor store, or even a grog-shop, so called, no more obstructs a public highway, than does a dry goods store, a jewelry store, or a butcher's shop.

Whatever poisons the air, or makes it either offensive or unhealthful, is a nuisance. But neither a hotel, nor a liquor store, nor a grog-shop poisons the air, or makes it offensive or unhealthful to outside persons.

Whatever obstructs the light, to which a man is legally entitled, is a nuisance. But neither a hotel, nor a liquor store, nor a grog-shop, obstructs anybody's light, except in cases where a church, a school-house, or a dwelling-house would have equally obstructed it. On this ground, therefore, the former are no more, and no less, nuisances than the latter would be.

Some persons are in the habit of saying that a liquor-shop is dangerous, in the same way that gunpowder is dangerous. But there is no analogy between the two cases. Gunpowder is liable to be exploded by accident, and especially by such fires as often occur in cities. For these reasons it is dangerous to persons and property in its immediate vicinity. But liquors are not liable to be thus exploded, and therefore are not dangerous nuisances, in any such sense as is gunpowder in cities.

But it is said, again, that drinking-places are frequently filled with noisy and boisterous men, who disturb the quiet of the neighborhood, and the sleep and rest of the neighbors.

*"An assembly of noisy drinkers is no more, and no less, a nuisance than is an assembly of shouting religious fanatics. Both of them are nuisances when they disturb the rest and sleep, or quiet, of neighbors."*

This may be true occasionally, though not very frequently. But whenever, in any case, it is true, the nuisance may be abated by the punishment of the proprietor and his customers, and if need be, by shutting up the place. But an assembly of noisy drinkers is no more a nuisance than is any other noisy assembly. A jolly or hilarious drinker disturbs the quiet

11

of a neighborhood no more, and no less, than does a shouting religious fanatic. An assembly of noisy drinkers is no more, and no less, a nuisance than is an assembly of shouting religious fanatics. Both of them are nuisances when they disturb the rest and sleep, or quiet, of neighbors. Even a dog that is given to barking, to the disturbance of the sleep or quiet of the neighborhood, is a nuisance.

## XIX.

BUT it is said, that for one person to entice another into a vice, is a crime.

This is preposterous. If any particular act is simply a vice, then a man who entices another to commit it, is simply an accomplice in the *vice*. He evidently commits no *crime*, because the accomplice can certainly commit no greater offence than the principal.

Every person who is sane, *compos mentis*, possessed of reasonable discretion and self-control, is presumed to be mentally competent to judge for himself of all the arguments, *pro and con*, that may be addressed to him, to persuade him to do any particular act; *provided no fraud is employed to deceive him.* And if he is persuaded or induced to do the act, his act is then his own; and even though the act prove to be harmful to himself, he cannot complain that the persuasion or arguments, to which he yielded his assent, were crimes against himself.

When fraud is practised, the case is, of course, different. If, for example, I offer a man poison, assuring him that it is a safe and wholesome drink, and he, on the faith of my assertion, swallows it, my act is a crime.

*"Volenti non fit injuria, is a maxim of the law. To the willing no injury is done. That is, no legal wrong."*

*Volenti non fit injuria*, is a maxim of the law. *To the willing no injury is done.* That is, no *legal* wrong. And every person who is sane, *compos mentis*, capable of exercising reasonable discretion in judging of the truth or falsehood of the representations or persuasions to which he yields his assent, *is* "willing," in the view of the law; and takes upon himself the entire responsibility for his acts, when no intentional fraud has been practised upon him.

This principle, *that to the willing no injury is done*, has no limit, except in the case of frauds, or of persons not possessed of reasonable discretion for judging in the particular case. If a person possessed of reasonable discretion, and not deceived by fraud, consents to practise the grossest vice, and thereby brings upon himself the greatest moral, physical, or pecuniary sufferings or losses, he cannot allege that he has been *legally* wronged. To illustrate this principle, take the case of rape. To have carnal knowledge of a woman, *against her will*, is the highest crime, next to murder, that can be committed against her. But to have carnal knowledge of her, *with her consent*, is no crime; but at most, a vice. And it is usually holden that a female child, of no more than *ten* years of age, has such reasonable discretion, that her consent, even though procured by rewards, or promises of reward, is sufficient to convert the act, which would otherwise be a high crime, into a simple act of vice.[2]

*"We see the same principle in the case of prize-fighters. If I but lay one of my fingers upon another man's person, against his will, no matter how lightly, and no matter how little practical injury is done, the act is a crime. But if two men agree to go out and pound each other's faces to a jelly, it is no crime, but only a vice. "*

We see the same principle in the case of prize-fighters. If I but lay one of my fingers upon another man's person, *against his will*, no matter how lightly, and no matter how little practical injury is done, the act is a crime. But if two men *agree* to go out and pound each other's faces to a jelly, it is no crime, but only a vice.

Even duels have not generally been considered crimes, because each man's life is his own, and the parties *agree* that each may take the other's life, if he can, by the use of such weapons as are agreed upon, and in conformity with certain rules that are also mutually assented to.

And this is a correct view of the matter, unless it can be said (as it probably cannot), that "anger is a madness" that so far deprives men of their reason as to make them incapable of reasonable discretion.

Gambling is another illustration of the principle that to the willing no injury is done. If I take but a single cent of a man's property, *without his consent*, the act is a crime. But if two men, who are *compos mentis*, possessed of reasonable discretion to judge of the nature and probable results of their act, sit down together, and each voluntarily stakes his money against the money of another, on the turn of a die, and one of them loses his whole estate (however large that may be), it is no crime, but only a vice.

*"It is not a crime, even, to assist a person to commit suicide, if he be in possession of his reason."*

It is not a crime, even, to assist a person to commit suicide, if he be in possession of his reason.

It is a somewhat common idea that suicide is, of itself, conclusive evidence of insanity. But, although it may ordinarily be very strong evidence of insanity, it is by no means conclusive in all cases. Many persons, in undoubted possession of their reason, have committed suicide, to escape the shame of a public exposure for their crimes, or to avoid some other great calamity. Suicide, in these cases, may not have been the highest wisdom, but it certainly was not proof of any lack of reasonable discretion.[3] And being within the limits of reasonable discretion, it was no crime for other persons to aid it, either by furnishing the instrument or otherwise. And if, in such cases, it be no crime to aid a suicide, how absurd to say that it is a crime to aid him in some act that is really pleasurable, and which a large portion of mankind have believed to be useful?

## XX.

BUT some persons are in the habit of saying that the use of spirituous liquors is *the* great source of crime; that "it fills our prisons with criminals;" and that this is reason enough for prohibiting the sale of them.

Those who say this, if they talk seriously, talk blindly and foolishly. They evidently mean to be understood as saying that a very large percentage of all the crimes that are committed among men, are committed by persons whose criminal passions are excited, *at the time*, by the use of liquors, and in consequence of the use of liquors.

This idea is utterly preposterous.

In the first place, the great crimes committed in the world are mostly prompted by avarice and ambition.

*"The greatest of all crimes are the wars that are carried on by governments, to plunder, enslave, and destroy mankind."*

The greatest of all crimes are the wars that are carried on by governments, to plunder, enslave, and destroy mankind.

*"The next greatest crimes committed in the world ... are committed, not so much by men who violate the laws, as by men who ... make the laws; by men who have combined to usurp arbitrary power, and to maintain it by force and fraud.... The robberies and wrongs thus committed by these men, in conformity with the laws,—that is, their own laws,—are as mountains to molehills, compared with the crimes committed by all other criminals, in violation of the laws."*

The next greatest crimes committed in the world are equally prompted by avarice and ambition; and are committed, not on sudden passion, but by men of calculation, who keep their heads cool and clear, and who have no thought whatever of going to prison for them. They are committed, not so much by men who *violate* the laws, as by men who, either by themselves or

13

by their instruments, *make* the laws; by men who have combined to usurp arbitrary power, and to maintain it by force and fraud, and whose purpose in usurping and maintaining it is, by unjust and unequal legislation, to secure to themselves such advantages and monopolies as will enable them to control and extort the labor and properties of other men, and thus impoverish them, in order to minister to their own wealth and aggrandizement.[4] The robberies and wrongs thus committed by these men, *in conformity with the laws,* that is, *their own laws,* are as mountains to molehills, compared with the crimes committed by all other criminals, in *violation* of the laws.

But, thirdly, there are vast numbers of frauds, of various kinds, committed in the transactions of trade, whose perpetrators, by their coolness and sagacity, evade the operation of the laws. And it is only their cool and clear heads that enable them to do it. Men under the excitement of intoxicating drinks are little disposed, and utterly unequal, to the successful practice of these frauds. They are the most incautious, the least successful, the least efficient, and the least to be feared, of all the criminals with whom the laws have to deal.

Fourthly. The professed burglars, robbers, thieves, forgers, counterfeiters, and swindlers, who prey upon society, are anything but reckless drinkers. Their business is of too dangerous a character to admit of such risks as they would thus incur.

Fifthly. The crimes that can be said to be committed under the influence of intoxicating drinks are mostly assaults and batteries, not very numerous, and generally not very aggravated. Some other small crimes, as petty thefts, or other small trespasses upon property, are sometimes committed, under the influence of drink, by feebleminded persons, not generally addicted to crime. The persons who commit these two kinds of crime are but few. They cannot be said to "fill our prisons;" or, if they do, we are to be congratulated that we need so few prisons, and so small prisons, to hold them.

The State of Massachusetts, for example, has a million and a half of people. How many of these are now in prison for *crimes*—not for the vice of intoxication, but for *crimes* committed against persons or property under the instigation of strong drink? I doubt if there be one in ten thousand, that is, one hundred and fifty in all; and the crimes for which these are in prison are mostly very small ones.

And I think it will be found that these few men are generally much more to be pitied than punished, for the reason that it was their poverty and misery, rather than any passion for liquor, or for crime, that led them to drink, and thus led them to commit their crimes under the influence of drink.

The sweeping charge that drink "fills our prisons with criminals" is made, I think, only by those men who know no better than to call a drunkard a criminal; and who have no better foundation for their charge than the shameful fact that we are such a brutal and senseless people, that we condemn and punish such weak and unfortunate persons as drunkards, as if they were criminals.

*"The legislators who authorize, and the judges who practise, such atrocities as these, are intrinsically criminals; unless their ignorance be such—as it probably is not—as to excuse them. And, if they were themselves to be punished as criminals, there would be more reason in our conduct."*

The legislators who authorize, and the judges who practise, such atrocities as these, are intrinsically criminals; unless their ignorance be such—as it probably is not—as to excuse them. And, if they were themselves to be punished as criminals, there would be more reason in our conduct.

A police judge in Boston once told me that he was in the habit of disposing of drunkards (by sending them to prison for thirty days—I think that was the stereotyped sentence) *at the rate of one in three minutes!* and sometimes more rapidly even than that; thus condemning them as criminals, and sending them to prison, without mercy, and without inquiry into circumstances, for an infirmity that entitled them to compassion and protection, instead of punishment. The real criminals in these cases were not the men who went to prison, but the judge, and the men behind him, who sent them there.

I recommend to those persons, who are so distressed lest the prisons of Massachusetts be filled with criminals, that they employ some portion, at least, of their philanthropy in preventing our prisons being filled with persons who are *not* criminals. I do not remember to have heard that their sympathies have ever been very actively exercised in that direction. On the contrary, they seem to have such a passion for punishing criminals, that they care not to inquire particularly whether a candidate for punishment really be a criminal. Such a passion, let me assure them, is a much more dangerous one, and one entitled to far less charity, both morally and legally, than the passion for strong drink.

It seems to be much more consonant with the merciless character of these men to send an unfortunate man to prison for drunkenness, and thus crush, and degrade, and dishearten him, and ruin him for life, than it does for them to lift him out of the poverty and misery that caused him to become a drunkard.

It is only those persons who have either little capacity, or little disposition, to enlighten, encourage, or aid mankind, that are possessed of this violent passion for governing, commanding, and punishing them. If, instead of standing by, and giving their consent and sanction to all the laws by which the weak man is first plundered, oppressed, and disheartened, and then punished as a criminal, they would turn their attention to the duty of defending his rights and improving his condition, and of thus strengthening him, and enabling him to stand on his own feet, and withstand the temptations that surround him, they would, I think, have little need to talk about laws and prisons for either rum-sellers or rum-drinkers, or even any other class of ordinary criminals. If, in short, these men, who are so anxious for the suppression of crime, would suspend, for a while, their calls upon the government for aid in suppressing the crimes of individuals, and would call upon the people for aid in suppressing the crimes of the government, they would show both their sincerity and good sense in a much stronger light than they do now. When the laws shall all be so just and equitable as to make it possible for all men and women to live honestly and virtuously, and to make themselves comfortable and happy, there will be much fewer occasions than now for charging them with living dishonestly and viciously.

## XXI.

BUT it will be said, again, that the use of spirituous liquors tends to poverty, and thus to make men paupers, and burdensome to the tax-payers; and that this is a sufficient reason why the sale of them should be prohibited.

There are various answers to this argument.

1. One answer is, that if the fact that the use of liquors tends to poverty and pauperism, be a sufficient reason for prohibiting the *sale* of them, it is equally a sufficient reason for prohibiting the *use* of them; for it is the *use*, and not the *sale*, that tends to poverty. The seller is, at most, merely an accomplice of the drinker. And it is a rule of law, as well as of reason, that if the principal in any act is not punishable, the accomplice cannot be.

2. A second answer to the argument is, that if government has the right, and is bound, to prohibit any one act—*that is not criminal* merely because it is supposed to tend to poverty, then, by the same rule, it has the right, and is bound, to prohibit any and every other act—*though not criminal* – which, in the opinion of the government, tends to poverty. And, on this principle, the government would not only have the right, *but would be bound*, to look into every man's private affairs, and every person's personal expenditures, and determine as to which of them did, and which of them did not, tend to poverty; and to prohibit and punish all of the former class. A man would have no right to expend a cent of his own property, according to his own pleasure or judgment, unless the legislature should be of the opinion that such expenditure would not tend to poverty.

3. A third answer to the same argument is, that if a man does bring himself to poverty, and even to beggary,—*either by his virtues or his vices,*—the government is under no obligation whatever to take care of him, unless it pleases to do so. It may let him perish in the street, or depend upon private charity, if it so pleases. It can carry out its own free will and discretion in the matter; for it is above all legal responsibility in such a case. It is not, *necessarily*, any part of a government's duty to provide for the poor. A government that is, a legitimate government is simply a voluntary association of individuals, who unite for such purposes, *and only for such purposes*, as suits them. If taking care of the poor whether they be virtuous or vicious be *not* one of those purposes, then the

government, *as a government*, has no more right, and is no more bound, to take care of them, than has or is a banking company, or a railroad company.

Whatever *moral* claims a poor man—whether he be virtuous or vicious—may have upon the charity of his fellow-men, he has no *legal* claims upon them. He must depend wholly upon their charity, if they so please. He cannot *demand*, as a *legal* right, that they either feed or clothe him. And he has no more *legal* or *moral* claims upon a government—which is but an association of individuals—than he has upon the same, or any other individuals, in their private capacity.

Inasmuch, then, as a poor man—whether virtuous or vicious—has no more or other claims, legal or moral, upon a government, for food or clothing, than he has upon private persons, a government has no more right than a private person to control or prohibit the expenditures or actions of an individual, on the ground that they tend to bring him to poverty.

Mr. A, *as an individual*, has clearly no right to prohibit any acts or expenditures of Mr. Z, through fear that such acts or expenditures may tend to bring him (Z) to poverty, and that he (Z) may, in consequence, at some future unknown time, come to him (A) in distress, and ask charity. And if A has no such right, *as an individual*, to prohibit any acts or expenditures on the part of Z, then government, which is a mere association of individuals, can have no such right.

Certainly no man, who is *compos mentis*, holds his right to the disposal and use of his own property, by any such worthless tenure as that which would authorize any or all of his neighbors,—whether calling themselves a government or not,—to interfere, and forbid him to make any expenditures, except such as *they* might think would *not* tend to poverty, and would *not* tend to ever bring him to them as a supplicant for their charity.

Whether a man, who is *compos mentis*, come to poverty, through his virtues or his vices, no man, nor body of men, can have any right to interfere with him, on the ground that their sympathy may some time be appealed to in his behalf; because, if it should be appealed to, they are at perfect liberty to act their own pleasure or discretion as to complying with his solicitations.

This right to refuse charity to the poor—whether the latter be virtuous or vicious—is one that governments always act upon. No government makes any more provision for the poor than it pleases. As a consequence, the poor are left, to a great extent, to depend upon private charity. In fact, they are often left to suffer sickness, and even death, because neither public nor private charity comes to their aid. How absurd, then, to say that government has a right to control a man's use of his own property, through fear that he may sometime come to poverty, and ask charity.

4. Still a fourth answer to the argument is, that the great and only incentive which each individual man has to labor, and to create wealth, is that he may dispose of it according to his own pleasure or discretion, and for the promotion of his own happiness, and the happiness of those whom he loves.[5]

Although a man may often, from inexperience or want of judgment, expend some portion of the products of his labor injudiciously, and so as not to promote his highest welfare, yet he learns wisdom in this, as in all other matters, by experience; by his mistakes as well as by his successes. *And this is the only way in which he can learn wisdom.* When he becomes convinced that he has made one foolish expenditure, he learns thereby not to make another like it. And he must be permitted to try his own experiments, and to try them to his own satisfaction, in this as in all other matters; for otherwise he has no motive to labor, or to create wealth at all.

> **"Any man, who is a man, would rather be a savage, and be free, ... than to be a civilized man, knowing how to create and accumulate wealth indefinitely, and yet not permitted to use or dispose of it, except under the supervision, direction, and dictation of a set of meddlesome, superserviceable fools and tyrants"**

Any man, who is a man, would rather be a savage, and be free, creating or procuring only such little wealth as he could control and consume from day to day, than to be a civilized man, knowing how to create and accumulate wealth indefinitely, and yet not permitted to use or dispose of it, except under the supervision, direction, and dictation of a set of meddlesome, superserviceable fools and tyrants, who, with no more knowledge than himself, and perhaps with not half so much, should assume to control him, on the ground that he had not the right, or the capacity, to determine for himself as to what he would do with the proceeds of his own labor.

5. A fifth answer to the argument is, that if it be the duty of government to watch over the expenditures of any one person, who is *compos mentis*, and not criminal, to see what ones tend to poverty, and what do not, and to prohibit and punish the former, then, by the same rule, it is bound to watch over the expenditures of all other persons, and prohibit and punish all that, in its judgment, tend to poverty.

If such a principle were carried out impartially, the result would be, that all mankind would be so occupied in watching each other's expenditures, and in testifying against, trying, and punishing such as tended to poverty, that they would have no time left to create wealth at all. Everybody capable of productive labor would either be in prison, or be acting as judge, juror, witness, or jailer. It would be impossible to create courts enough to try, or to build prisons enough to hold, the offenders. All productive labor would cease; and the fools that were so intent on preventing poverty, would not only all come to poverty, imprisonment, and starvation themselves, but would bring everybody else to poverty, imprisonment, and starvation.

6. If it be said that a man may, at least, be rightfully compelled to support his family, and, consequently, to abstain from all expenditures that, in the opinion of the government, tend to disable him to perform that duty, various answers might be given. But this one is sufficient, viz.: that no man, unless a fool or a slave, would acknowledge any family to be his, if that acknowledgment were to be made an excuse, by the government, for depriving him, either of his personal liberty, or the control of his property.

When a man is allowed his natural liberty, and the control of his property, his family is usually, almost universally, the great paramount object of his pride and affection; and he will, not only voluntarily, but as his highest pleasure, employ his best powers of mind and body, not merely to provide for them the ordinary necessaries and comforts of life, but to lavish upon them all the luxuries and elegancies that his labor can procure.

A man enters into no moral or legal obligation with his wife or chidren to do anything for them, except what he can do consistently with his own personal freedom, and his natural right to control his own property at his own discretion.

If a government can step in and say to a man, who is *compos mentis*, and who is doing his duty to his family, *as he sees his duty*, and according to *his* best judgment, however imperfect that may be, "We (the government) suspect that you are not employing your labor to the best advantage for your family; *we* suspect that your expenditures, and your disposal of your property, are not so judicious as they might be, for the interest of your family; and therefore *we* (the government) will take you and your property under our special surveillance, and prescribe to you what you may, and may not do, with yourself and your property; and your family shall hereafter look to *us* (the government), and not to you, for support" if a government can do this, all a man's pride, ambition, and affection, relative to his family, would be crushed, so far as it would be possible for human tyranny to crush them; and he would either never have a family (whom he would publicly acknowledge to be his), or he would risk both his property and his life in overthrowing such an insulting, outrageous, and insufferable tyranny. And any woman who would wish her husband—he being *compos mentis* to submit to such an unnatural insult and wrong, is utterly undeserving of his affection, or of anything but his disgust and contempt. And he would probably very soon cause her to understand that, if she chose to rely on the government, for the support of herself and her children, rather than on him, she must rely on the government alone.

## XXII.

STILL another and all-sufficient answer to the argument that the use of spirituous liquors tends to poverty, is that, *as a general rule*, it puts the effect before the cause. It assumes that it is the use of the liquors that causes the poverty, instead of its being the poverty that causes the use of the liquors.

Poverty is the natural parent of nearly all the ignorance, vice, crime, and misery there are in the world.[6]

Why is it that so large a portion of the laboring people of England are drunken and vicious? Certainly not because they are by nature any worse than other men. But it is because their extreme and hopeless poverty keeps them in ignorance and servitude, destroys their courage and self-respect, subjects them to such constant insults and wrongs, to such incessant and bitter miseries of every kind, and finally drives them to such despair, that the short respite that drink or other vice affords them, is, for the time being, a relief. This is the chief cause of the drunkenness and other vices that prevail among the laboring people of England.

If those laborers of England, who are now drunken and vicious, had had the same chances and surroundings in life as the more fortunate classes have had; if they had been reared in comfortable, and happy, and virtuous homes, instead of squalid, and wretched, and vicious ones; if they had had opportunities to acquire knowledge and property, and make themselves intelligent, comfortable, happy, independent, and respected, and to secure to themselves all the intellectual, social, and domestic enjoyments which honest and justly rewarded industry could enable them to secure, if they could have had all this, instead of being born to a life of hopeless, unrewarded toil, with a certainty of death in the workhouse, they would have been as free from their present vices and weaknesses as those who reproach them now are.

It is of no use to say that drunkenness, or any other vice, only adds to their miseries; for such is human nature the weakness of human nature, if you please that men can endure but a certain amount of misery, before their hope and courage fail, and they yield to almost anything that promises present relief or mitigation; though at the cost of still greater misery in the future. To preach morality or temperance to such wretched persons, instead of relieving their sufferings, or improving their conditions, is only insulting their wretchedness.

Will those who are in the habit of attributing men's poverty to their vices, instead of their vices to their poverty,—as if every poor person, or most poor persons, were specially vicious,—tell us whether all the poverty and want that, within the last year and a half,*[7] have been brought so suddenly--as it were in a moment upon at least twenty millions of the people of the United States, were brought upon them as a natural consequence, either of their drunkenness, or of any other of their vices? Was it their drunkenness, or any other of their vices, that paralyzed, as by a stroke of lightning, all the industries by which they lived, and which had, but a few days before, been in such prosperous activity? Was it their vices that turned the adult portion of those twenty millions out of doors without employment, compelled them to consume their little accumulations, if they had any, and then to become beggars, beggars for work, and, failing in this, beggars for bread? Was it their vices that, all at once, and without warning, filled the homes of so many of them with want, misery, sickness, and death? No. Clearly it was neither the drunkenness, nor any other vices, of these laboring people, that brought upon them all this ruin and wretchedness. And if it was not, *what was it?*

This is the problem that must be answered; for it is one that is repeatedly occurring, and constantly before us, and that cannot be put aside.

In fact, the poverty of the great body of mankind, the world over, is the great problem of the world. That such extreme and nearly universal poverty exists all over the world, and has existed through all past generations, proves that it originates in causes which the common human nature of those who suffer from it, has not hitherto been strong enough to overcome. But these sufferers are, at least, beginning to see these causes, and are becoming resolute to remove them, let it cost what it may. And those who imagine that they have nothing to do but to go on attributing the poverty of the poor to their vices, and preaching to them against their vices, will ere long wake up to find that the day for all such talk is past. And the question will then be, not what are men's vices, but what are their rights?

*"the poverty of the great body of mankind ... is the great problem of the world. ... And those who ... attribut(e) the poverty of the poor to their vices, and preaching to them against their vices, will ere long wake up to find that the day for all such talk is past. And the question will then be, not what are men's vices, but what are their rights?"*

18

## Notes

[1] To give an insane man a knife, or any other weapon, or thing, by which he is likely to injure himself, is a crime.

[2] The statute book of Massachusetts makes ten years the age at which a female child is supposed to have discretion enough to part with her virtue. But the same statute book holds that no person, man or woman, of any age, or any degree of wisdom or experience, has discretion enough to be trusted to buy and drink a glass of spirits, on his or her own judgment! What an illustration of the legislative wisdom of Massachusetts!

[3] Cato committed suicide to avoid falling into the hands of Cæsar. Who ever suspected that he was insane? Brutus did the same. Colt committed suicide only an hour or so before he was to be hanged. He did it to avoid bringing upon his name and his family the disgrace of having it said that he was hanged. This, whether a really wise act or not, was clearly an act within reasonable discretion. Does any one suppose that the person who furnished him with the necessary instrument was a criminal?

[4] An illustration of this fact is found in England, whose government, for a thousand years and more, has been little or nothing else than a band of robbers, who have conspired to monopolize the land, and, as far as possible, all other wealth. These conspirators, calling themselves kings, nobles, and freeholders, have, by force and fraud, taken to themselves all civil and military power; they keep themselves in power solely by force and fraud, and the corrupt use of their wealth; and they employ their power solely in robbing and enslaving the great body of their own people, and in plundering and enslaving other peoples. And the world has been, and now is, full of examples substantially similar. And the governments of our own country do not differ so widely from others, in this respect, as some of us imagine.

[5] It is to this incentive alone that we are indebted for all the wealth that has ever been created by human labor, and accumulated for the benefit of mankind.

[6] Except those great crimes, which the few, calling themselves governments, practise upon the many, by means of organized, systematic extortion and tyranny. And it is only the poverty, ignorance, and consequent weakness of the many, that enable the combined and organized few to acquire and maintain such arbitrary power over them.

[7] That is, from September 1, 1873, to March 1, 1875.

19

## Further Information

SOURCE

The edition used for this extract: Lysander Spooner, *The Shorter Works and Pamphlets of Lysander Spooner, vol. 2 (1862-1884)* (Indianapolis: Liberty Fund, 2010). "Vices are Not Crimes: A Vindication of Moral Liberty." <oll.libertyfund.org/title/2292/217204>.

Copyright: The text is in the public domain.

FURTHER READING

Other works by Lysander Spooner (1808-1887) <oll.libertyfund.org/person/4664>.

School of Thought: 19th Century Natural Rights Theorists <oll.libertyfund.org/collection/38>.

*"The distinctive principle of Western social philosophy is individualism. It aims at the creation of a sphere in which the individual is free to think, to choose, and to act without being restrained by the interference of the social apparatus of coercion and oppression, the State."*

*[Ludwig von Mises, "Liberty and Property" (1958)]*

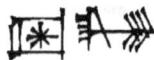

### ABOUT THE BEST OF THE OLL

*The Best of the Online Library of Liberty* is a collection of some of the most important material in the Online Library of Liberty. They are chapter length extracts which have been formatted as pamphlets in **PDF, ePub**, and **Kindle** formats for easier distribution. These extracts are designed for use in the classroom and discussion groups, or material for a literature table for outreach. The full list can be found here <oll.libertyfund.org/title/2465>.

Another useful sampling of the contents of the OLL website is the collection of weekly *Quotations about Liberty and Power* which are organized by themes such as Free Trade, Money and Banking, Natural Rights, and so on. See for example, Richard Cobden's "I have a dream" speech <oll.libertyfund.org/quote/326>.

### ABOUT THE OLL AND LIBERTY FUND

The *Online Library of Liberty* is a project of Liberty Fund, Inc., a private educational foundation established in 1960 to encourage the study of the ideal of a society of free and responsible individuals. The OLL website has a large collection of books and study guides about individual liberty, limited constitutional government, the free market, and peace.

Liberty Fund: <www.libertyfund.org>.

OLL: <oll.libertyfund.org>.

.